Guess What!

Student's Book 3B

Susannah Reed with Kay Bentley
Series Editor: Lesley Koustaff

CAMBRIDGE
UNIVERSITY PRESS

Contents

			Page
5 **Home time**			58
Vocabulary	drink juice, eat a sandwich, do the dishes, play on the computer, read a book, watch TV, do homework, listen to music, make a cake, wash the car		60
Grammar	He (doesn't like) (reading books). ● Does he (enjoy) (doing the dishes)? Yes, he does. / No, he doesn't.		61–62
Skills	Listening ● Are you helpful at home?		63
Story value	Show forgiveness		64
Talk time	Suggesting food to make	**Say it!** *th* ● panthers, three	65
CLIL: Geography	Where do people live?		66–67
6 **Hobbies**			68
Vocabulary	play the piano, play the guitar, play the recorder, make models, make movies, do karate, do gymnastics, play Ping-Pong, play badminton, play volleyball		70
Grammar	She (does karate) (on Sundays). ● Does she (do gymnastics) (in the evening)? Yes, she does. / No, she doesn't.		71–72
Skills	Reading ● What sports do you like?		73
Story value	Try new things		74
Talk time	Encouraging others to try things	**Say it!** *sh* ● sharks, fish	75
CLIL: Music	What type of musical instrument is it?		76–77
Review	Units 5 and 6		78–79
7 **At the market**			80
Vocabulary	lemons, limes, watermelons, coconuts, grapes, mangoes, pineapples, pears, tomatoes, onions		82
Grammar	There (are lots of) (grapes). ● There (are some) (tomatoes). ● There (aren't any) (limes). ● Are there any (pears)? Yes, there are. / No, there aren't.		83–84
Skills	Listening ● Do you like smoothies?		85
Story value	Reuse old things		86
Talk time	Making choices	**Say it!** *ch* ● chipmunks, pouches	87
CLIL: Science	What parts of plants can we eat?		88–89
8 **At the beach**			90
Vocabulary	sun, burger, fries, sunglasses, swimsuit, shorts, towel, shell, ocean, sand		92
Grammar	Which (towel) is (theirs)? The (purple) one. ● Whose (jacket) is this? It's (mine). Whose (shoes) are these? They're (Sally's).		93–94
Skills	● Reading ● What do you like doing on vacation?		95
Story value	Appreciate your family and friends		96
Talk time	Deciding how to travel	**Say it!** *ph / f* ● dolphins, fish	97
CLIL: Math	Are sea animals symmetrical?		98–99
Review	Units 7 and 8		100–101
Chants			102

5 Home time

Guess What!

59

1 **CD2 02** Listen and point.

2 **CD2 03** Listen, point, and repeat.

3 **CD2 04** Listen and answer the questions.

1. Is he drinking juice?   Yes, he is.

4 **Think** Describe and guess the numbers.

She's making a cake.   Number 9!

1. drink juice
2. eat a sandwich
3. do the dishes
4. play on the computer
5. read a book
6. watch TV
7. do homework
8. listen to music
9. make a cake
10. wash the car

→ Workbook page 48

5 (CD2 05) Sing the song.

We are all different,
In my family.
We are all different,
My family and me.

I like listening to music,
But I don't like reading books.
My mom loves reading books,
But she doesn't like watching TV.

My sister enjoys watching TV,
But she doesn't like making cakes.
My dad loves making cakes,
But he doesn't like listening to music.

6 Make sentences about the song and say who.

He enjoys listening to music.   Alex!

7 (About Me) Ask and answer with your friend. Then tell another friend.

Do you like playing on the computer?

Yes, I do. I love playing on the computer.

Ellie loves playing on the computer.

Remember!

He **likes** listening to music.
He **doesn't like** reading books.
She **enjoys** watching TV.
She **loves** playing on the computer.

8 (CD2 06) **Look at the photographs and choose. Then listen and repeat.**

1

Does he like playing on the computer?
Yes, he does. / No, he doesn't.

2

Does she enjoy washing the car?
Yes, she does. / No, she doesn't.

9 (CD2 07) **Listen and find. Then answer the question.**

Pedro   Vivian   Fred
Lina
Anil   Camilla

10 **Ask and answer with a friend.**

Does Lina like doing homework?   Yes, she does.

11 (CD2 08) **Go to page 102. Listen and repeat the chant.**

Remember!
Does he enjoy doing the dishes?
Yes, he **does**.   No, he **doesn't**.

Skills: *Listening and speaking*

 Let's start! **Are you helpful at home?**

12 (CD2 09) **Listen and choose.**

1 Isabella **likes / doesn't like** cleaning her bedroom.
2 She **enjoys / doesn't enjoy** washing the car.
3 She **likes / doesn't like** doing the dishes.
4 Brad **likes / doesn't like** cleaning his bedroom.
5 He **enjoys / doesn't enjoy** washing his bike.
6 He **enjoys / doesn't enjoy** making cakes.

Brad

Isabella

13 (About Me) **Ask and answer with a friend.**

Do you like cleaning your bedroom?
Do you like washing the car?
Do you like doing the dishes?
Do you like making cakes?

Writing

➡ Workbook page 51: Write about being helpful at home.

14 CD2 10 **Read and listen.**

Value: Show forgiveness → Workbook page 52

Listen and repeat. Then act.

chocolate cake   cheese sandwich   carrot cake
sausage sandwich   chicken sandwich

1

Let's make a **carrot cake**.

What do we need?

Eggs, milk, carrots ...

OK. Here we are.

2

Let's make a **chicken sandwich**.

What do we need?

Bread, chicken ...

Say it!

16 CD2 12 Listen and repeat.

Panthers learn to hunt three months after birth.

panthers

Where do **people** live?

1 CD2 13 Listen and repeat.

countryside

village

town

city

2 Watch the video.

3 What can you see in the pictures?

Guess What!

There are more chickens in the world than people.

Project

5 Make a mind map for a town or a city.

Supermarkets, big movie theaters, hospitals, police stations, and stores and fire stations
Clothes for
Hospital
City of Seville
girls and boys
trains, cars and buses

4 Where would you like to live?

CLIL: Geography **67**

Guess What!

1 (CD2 14) **Listen and point.**

2 (CD2 15) **Listen, point, and repeat.**

Weekend Clubs and Activities

music clubs

craft clubs

sports clubs

3 (CD2 16) **Listen and say the numbers.**

4 (Think) **Ask questions and guess the numbers.**

Is he playing the piano?   No, he isn't.

Is he making a model?   Yes, he is.

Number 4!

1 play the piano
2 play the guitar
3 play the recorder
4 make models
5 make movies
6 do karate
7 do gymnastics
8 play Ping-Pong
9 play badminton
10 play volleyball

5 (CD2 17) Sing the song.

This is our friend Lizzie.
She's very busy!

She plays badminton on Saturdays,
And she does karate on Sundays.
She makes models after school on Wednesdays,
And she makes movies on Mondays.

She doesn't play on the computer,
And she doesn't watch TV after school.
She plays the guitar in the morning,
And she plays the piano in the afternoon.

We like our friend Lizzie.
She's very busy!

6 Make sentences about the song. Say *true* or *false*.

Lizzie doesn't play badminton on Saturdays.   False!

7 (About Me) Ask and answer with your friend. Then tell another friend.

Do you do karate?

Yes, I do. I do karate on Saturdays.

Sam does karate on Saturdays.

Remember!

She **does** karate on Sundays.
She **doesn't watch** TV after school.
She **plays** the guitar in the morning.

8 (CD2 18) **Look and choose. Then listen and repeat.**

1

Jimmy –
Don't forget tennis club on Tuesday.

> Does he play tennis on Tuesdays?
> Yes, he does. / No, he doesn't.

2

Leah – Remember volleyball club after school.

> Does she play volleyball in the morning?
> Yes, she does. / No, she doesn't.

9 (CD2 19) **Listen and answer the questions.**

10 (About Me) **Ask and answer about your friends.**

Does George do karate after school?   Yes, he does.

11 (CD2 20) **Go to page 102. Listen and repeat the chant.**

Remember!

Does she do gymnastics in the evening?
Yes, she does.   No, she doesn't.

Skills: *Reading and speaking*

 Let's start! **What sports do you like?**

12 (CD2 21) **Read and listen. Then match.**

a

Sports we like

Meet Josh. He's ten years old, and he wants to be a soccer player.

Josh goes to a soccer club on Tuesdays and Thursdays after school. He plays soccer on Saturdays and Sundays, too. Josh also plays basketball, and he goes swimming.

Josh has a healthy diet. His favorite dinner is chicken with potatoes or rice and vegetables. He likes fruit, too. His favorite drink is a banana milkshake!

b

13 **Read again and answer the questions.**

1 What club does Josh go to?
2 Does he play soccer on Saturdays?
3 Does he play other sports?
4 Does he eat fruits and vegetables?

14 (About Me) **Ask and answer with a friend.**

Do you go to a club after school?
What sports do you play?
Do you have a healthy diet?
Which fruits and vegetables do you like?

Writing

➔ Workbook page 59: Write about your favorite sport.

16 **Listen and repeat. Then act.**

play the guitar   make models   do gymnastics
do karate   play Ping-Pong

Do you want to play Ping-Pong with me?

No, sorry. I can't play Ping-Pong.

Come on – try it!

OK.

Say it!

17 **Listen and repeat.**

Sharks are fish with sharp teeth.

shark

What type of **musical instrument** is it?

1 (CD2 25) **Listen and repeat.**

brass   percussion   string   woodwind   piano

2 **Watch the video.**

3 **What type of musical instruments can you see?**

Guess What!

A piano is a string instrument and a percussion instrument.

Project

5 **Make a drum from recycled cardboard.**

4 **What type of instrument would you like to play?**

Review

Units 5 and 6

1 Find the words in the puzzles and match to the photographs.

od scitsanmyg

yalp llabyellov

tae a hciwdnas

netsil ot cisum

Kiki

2 CD2 26 Listen and say the names.

3 Read and say the names.

1 She likes listening to music.
2 He goes to gymnastics club on Tuesdays.
3 She plays volleyball after school.
4 He likes eating sandwiches.

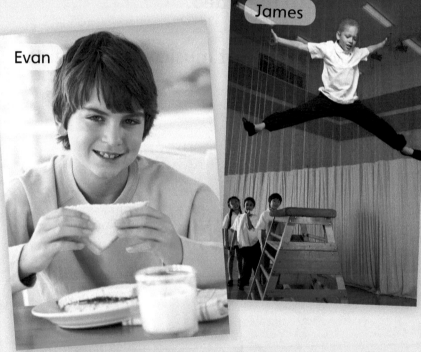
Evan
James

4 Make your own word puzzles for your friend.

Choose indoor or outdoor activities:
hsaw eht rac
ekam a ekac

Clara

→ Workbook pages 64–65

5 Play the game.

79

Guess What!

1 〔CD2 27〕 **Listen and point.**

2 〔CD2 28〕 **Listen, point, and repeat.**

3 〔CD2 29〕 **Listen and say the fruits and vegetables.**

4 〔Think〕 **Describe and guess what.**

These fruits are small and yellow.　　Lemons!

1 lemons
2 limes
3 watermelons
4 coconuts
5 grapes
6 mangoes
7 pineapples
8 pears
9 tomatoes
10 onions

5 (CD2 30) Sing the song.

Come and buy some fruit
At my market stall today!

There are lots of pineapples,
And there are some pears,
But there aren't any mangoes
At your market stall today.

Come and buy some fruit
At my market stall today!

There are lots of lemons,
And there are some limes,
But there aren't any tomatoes
At your market stall today.

6 Look at the song and find the differences in this picture.

There are lots of grapes.

7 (About Me) Say what you can buy in your town market.

There are lots of lemons in my town market.

Remember!

There are lots of grapes.
There are some tomatoes.
There aren't any limes.

8 CD2 31 **Listen and repeat.**

Are there any onions?

Yes, there are.

Are there any coconuts?

No, there aren't.

9 Think **Look at the picture. Then cover it and play a memory game.**

mangoes
coconuts
apples
pineapples
watermelons
carrots
onions
beans
limes
lemons
pears
tomatoes

Are there any mangoes?

No, there aren't.

10 About Me **Ask and answer about your classroom.**

Are there any books?

Yes, there are.

Remember!

Are there any pears?
Yes, there are.
No, there aren't.

11 CD2 32 **Go to page 102. Listen and repeat the chant.**

Skills: *Listening and speaking*

 Let's start! **Do you like smoothies?**

12 (CD2 33) **Listen and say the numbers.**

1
Mango Cooler with ...
Banana
Mango
Orange juice

2
Tropical Mix with ...
Pineapple
Banana
Orange juice

Smoothie café

3
Tutti Frutti with ...
Pineapple
Grapes
Watermelon

13 (CD2 33) **Listen again and answer the questions.**

1 Does Emilio like bananas?
2 What are Arianna's favorite fruit?
3 Does Marco like orange juice?

14 (About Me) **Ask and answer with a friend.**

What is your favorite smoothie?
What is your favorite fruit?
Which smoothie don't you like?
Which fruit don't you like?

Writing

 Workbook page 69: Write about your favorite smoothie.

Listen and repeat. Then act.

| brown watch | red purse | blue guitar | white radio |

Which watch do you want?

The brown one, please.

OK. Here you are.

Say it!

17 Listen and repeat.

Chipmunks have big cheek pouches.

chipmunk

What parts of plants can we eat?

1 (CD2 37) Listen and repeat.

2 Watch the video.

3 Match the fruits and vegetables with the plant parts.

5 fruit
4 leaf
3 stem
2 root
1 seed

roots
stems
leaves
fruit
seeds

Guess What!

Some plants eat small frogs and lizards.

Project

5 Write a menu using the five parts of plants we can eat.

Starter
Main
Leaf stem root
Dessert
fruit

4 What plants do you like to eat?

8 At the beach

Guess What!

1 (CD2 38) **Listen and point.**

2 (CD2 39) **Listen, point, and repeat.**

3 (CD2 40) **Listen and say the words.**

4 (Think) **Make sentences and guess what.**

Lucas is wearing these. They're black.   Sunglasses!

1 sun
2 burger
3 fries
4 sunglasses
5 swimsuit
6 shorts
7 towel
8 shell
9 ocean
10 sand

5 CD2 41 Sing the song.

Which hat is yours?
The red one's mine.
Which hat is yours?
The blue one.

Which sock is hers?
The green one's hers.
Which sock is his?
The yellow one.

Which towel is ours?
The pink one's ours.
Which towel is theirs?
The purple one.

6 Look at the song. Then read and match.

1 Which towel is ours?

2 Which sock is hers?

3 Which hat is yours?

4 Which sock is his?

5 Which towel is theirs?

a The green one's hers.   **b** The yellow one's his.   **c** The blue one's mine.

d The purple one.   **e** The pink one.

7 Ask and answer about your classroom.

Which pencil case is yours?

The purple one's mine.

Remember!
Which sock is hers?
The green one's hers.
Which towel is theirs?
The purple one.

8 CD2 42 **Listen and repeat.**

Whose jacket is this?

It's mine.

Whose shoes are these?

They're Sally's.

9 About Me **Find these things in your classroom. Then ask and answer.**

Whose backpack is this?

It's Mark's.

10 CD2 43 **Go to page 102. Listen and repeat the chant.**

Remember!

Whose glasses are these?
They're mine.

Skills: *Reading and speaking*

 What do you like doing on vacation?

11 CD2 44 **Read and listen. Then match.**

a

Dear Grandma and Grandpa,

We're having a great vacation. Can you see the hotel next to the beach? That's ours!

The beach is great. We like playing in the sand. There are lots of shells. We like making pictures with them.

In the evening, we go to the café on the beach. You can see it in this photograph. I like eating a burger and fries. They're delicious!

See you soon!

Love from Louis

b

12 **Read and say *true* or *false*.**

1 Their hotel is next to a forest.
2 They like playing on the beach.
3 There aren't any shells on the beach.
4 Louis likes eating chicken and fries.

13 About Me **Ask and answer with a friend.**

Where do you like going on vacation?
Who do you go on vacation with?
What do you do on vacation?
What do you like eating on vacation?

Writing

 Workbook page 77: Write a postcard to a friend.

15   **Listen and repeat. Then act.**

| by plane | by bike | on foot | by train | by car | by bus |

1

How should we get to the movie theater?

Let's go by car.

OK. Good idea.

2

How should we get to the beach?

Let's go by bus.

No, let's go by train!

Say it!

16   **Listen and repeat.**

Dolphins are friendly and eat fish.

dolphins

Are sea animals symmetrical?

1 (CD2 48) Listen and repeat.

1 starfish 2 crab 3 jellyfish 4 octopus 5 sea horse

2 Watch the video.

3 In these pictures, which sea animals are symmetrical?

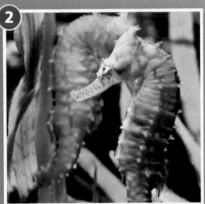

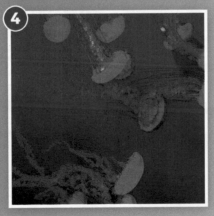

Guess What!

Starfish and octopuses can grow new legs.

Project

5 Make a poster with symmetrical sea animals.

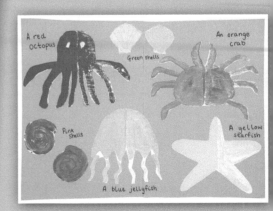

A red octopus Green shells An orange crab Pink shells A blue jellyfish A yellow starfish

4 Which sea animals do you like?

Review

Units 7 and 8

1 Find the words and match to the photographs.

mangoesshellsoceansunglasses

2 CD2 49 Listen and say the numbers.

3 Answer the questions.

1 Where are Aiden and his sister playing?
2 Whose shells are on the beach?
3 Are there any mangoes on the beach?
4 Are there any sunglasses at the market?

4 Make your own word puzzles for your friend.

Choose fruits or vegetables:
lemonslimespears

Start

Is there a gym in Lucas's school?
(See Unit 2)

Whose painting is this?

Are there any apples at the market?
(See Unit 7)

Whose presents are these?

Are there any animals in Lucas's yard?
(See Unit 1)

Whose tiger is this?

Are there any shells at the beach?
(See Unit 8)

Whose dog is this?

#1

Whose sunglasses are these?

Are there any butterflies in the park?
(See Unit 1)

Whose aunt is this?

Is there a computer at Tom's house?
(See Unit 5)

Start

Chants

Unit 5 (page 62)

 Listen and repeat the chant.

Does he like playing on the computer?
Yes, he does. Yes, he does.
Does she enjoy washing the car?
No, she doesn't. No, she doesn't.

Does she like doing homework?
Yes, she does. Yes, she does.
Does he enjoy reading books?
No, he doesn't. No, he doesn't.

Unit 6 (page 72)

 Listen and repeat the chant.

Does he play tennis on Tuesdays?
Yes, he does. Yes, he does.
Does she play volleyball in the morning?
No, she doesn't. No, she doesn't.

Does he do karate after school?
Yes, he does. Yes, he does.
Does she do gymnastics in the evening?
No, she doesn't. No, she doesn't.

Unit 7 (page 84)

11 **Listen and repeat the chant.**

Are there any onions?
Yes, there are. Yes, there are.
Are there any coconuts?
No, there aren't. No, there aren't.

Are there any pears?
Yes, there are. Yes, there are.
Are there any mangoes?
No, there aren't. No, there aren't.

Unit 8 (page 94)

10 **Listen and repeat the chant.**

Whose jacket is this?
It's mine. It's mine.
Whose shoes are these?
They're Sally's.

Whose backpack is this?
It's Mark's. It's Mark's.
Whose glasses are these?
They're mine.

Workbook **3B**

with Online Resources

Contents

		Page
Unit 5	Home time	48
Unit 6	Hobbies	56
Review	Units 5–6	64
Unit 7	At the market	66
Unit 8	At the beach	74
Review	Units 7–8	82
My picture dictionary		84
My puzzle		88

Lynne Marie Robertson

Series Editor: Lesley Koustaff

CAMBRIDGE
UNIVERSITY PRESS

5 Home time

1 Look and match.

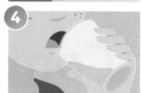

a listen to music

b eat a sandwich

c do the dishes

d read a book

e drink juice

f make a cake

g watch TV

h wash the car

2 Look at activity 1. Complete the sentences.

1 Look at picture 1.   He's *reading a book* .

2 Look at picture 2.   He's _____ .

3 Look at picture 4.   She's _____ .

4 Look at picture 6.   She's _____ .

5 Look at picture 7.   He's _____ .

3 (About Me) Answer the questions.

1 Do you like listening to music? _____

2 Do you like playing on the computer? _____

3 Do you like doing homework? _____

My picture dictionary → Go to page 84: Find and write the new words.

4 **Read and match.**

1 I love making cakes. ←

2 My mom likes listening to music.

3 My sister enjoys doing homework.

4 My brother doesn't enjoy playing
   this game on the computer.

5 My dad doesn't like doing the dishes.

5 (Think) **Look and complete the sentences.**

| like   love   doesn't enjoy   doesn't like | drink   read   wash   watch |

He _doesn't like drinking_ juice.

She _____ books.

He _____ TV.

She _____ the car.

6 **Write about your friend.**

Name: _My friend's name_ _____

1 _____ loves _____ .

2 _____ likes _____ .

3 _____ doesn't enjoy _____ .

7 Look and complete the questions. Then circle the answers.

1 Does he like _____reading books_____ ? (Yes, he does.) / No, he doesn't.
2 Does she enjoy _____ ? Yes, she does. / No, she doesn't.
3 Does she like _____ ? Yes, she does. / No, she doesn't.
4 Does he like _____ ? Yes, he does. / No, he doesn't.
5 Does he enjoy _____ ? Yes, he does. / No, he doesn't.
6 Does she like _____ ? Yes, she does. / No, she doesn't.

8 (Think) Look and complete the questions and answers. Then draw.

Does she enjoy ___making___ a cake?
No, ___she doesn't___ .

_____ enjoy _____ TV?
No, _____ .

_____ love _____
on the computer?
Yes, _____ .

_____ like _____
homework?
Yes, _____ .

Skills: *Writing*

9 **Read the paragraph and write the words.**

love eating   enjoy cleaning   don't like doing   enjoy washing   ~~like making~~

I'm helpful at home. In the morning, I ¹___*like making*___ cakes, and I
²_____ them! I ³_____ my bedroom, too. In the
afternoon, I'm helpful. I ⁴_____ the dog or the car. After dinner,
I'm not helpful. I ⁵_____ the dishes!

10 (About Me) **Answer the questions.**

1   What do you enjoy cleaning?
   *I enjoy*_____

2   What do you like washing?
_____

3   What do you like making?
_____

4   What do you love doing?
_____

5   What don't you like doing?
_____

11 (About Me) **Write about being helpful at home.**

*I'm helpful at home. I like*_____
_____
_____
_____
_____

12 (About Me) **Ask and answer with a friend.**

Do you like cleaning your bedroom?   Yes, I do.

13 **Read and write the words.**

need   Watch out   so sorry   ~~likes making~~

a
My Aunt Pat _likes making_ cakes.

Find a chocolate cake.

Great! Let's go to her house!

b
What do we _____ ?

Eggs, milk, chocolate …

c
_____ , Lucas!

Oh, no!

d
Oh, dear! I'm _____ .

Me, too!

14 **Look at activity 13. Answer the questions.**

1   Where are the children going?   _Aunt Pat's house._

2   Does Aunt Pat like making cakes?   _____

3   What do they need to make the cake?   _____

4   What does Lucas drop?   _____

5   Who's sorry?   _____

15 Look and check the picture that shows the value: show forgiveness.

16 Color the words that sound like tee*th*. Then answer the question.

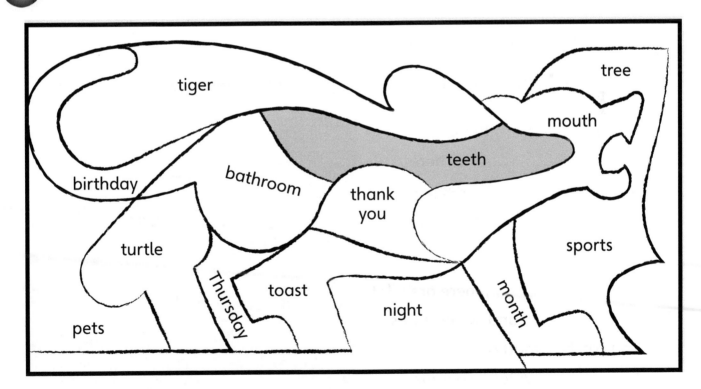

What's this animal? _____

Where do people live?

1 Find the words and write under the pictures.

wont~~ llivgea   ytic   ouidecyrtns

town

2 Look and complete the sentences.

café   houses   riding   stores   supermarket   town   ~~village~~   walking

In the ¹___village___ there
is a small ²_____ . There
are two ³_____ . People
like ⁴_____ their bikes there.

In the ⁵_____ , there are a lot
of ⁶_____ and some stores.
You can buy food at the
⁷_____ . A lot of people
are ⁸_____ in the street.

Evaluation

1 **Read and match. Then answer the questions.**

Tom

1 read a book

2 do the dishes

3 do homework

4 listen to music

5 make a cake

6 drink juice

Cara

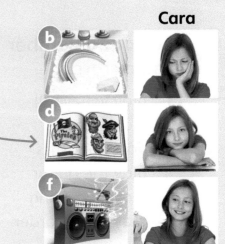

1 Does she like reading a book?   _Yes, she does._
2 Does she love doing the dishes?   _____
3 Does he like doing homework?   _____
4 Does he enjoy drinking juice?   _____

2 **Look at activity 1. Complete the sentences.**

1 Tom enjoys _doing homework_ .
2 Tom loves _____ , but he doesn't like _____ .
3 Cara loves _____ .
4 Cara doesn't enjoy _____ , but she likes _____ .

3 About Me **Complete the sentences about this unit.**

1 I can talk about _____ .

2 I can write about _____ .

3 My favorite part is _____ .

4 Puzzle **Guess what it is.**

Go to page 88 and circle the answer.

55

6 Hobbies

1 Look and number the picture.

1 play volleyball
2 make movies
3 do gymnastics
4 play the guitar
5 play Ping-Pong
6 play the recorder

2 Look and write the words.

| make | do | ~~play~~ | play | | models | ~~badminton~~ | the piano | karate |

1. play
   badminton

2. _____

3. _____

4. _____

3 Write the words from activities 1 and 2 on the lists.

Crafts

make movies

_____

_____

Music

_____

_____

_____

Sports

_____

_____

_____

My picture dictionary → Go to page 85: Find and write the new words.

4 Think **Look and follow. Then write *true* or *false*.**

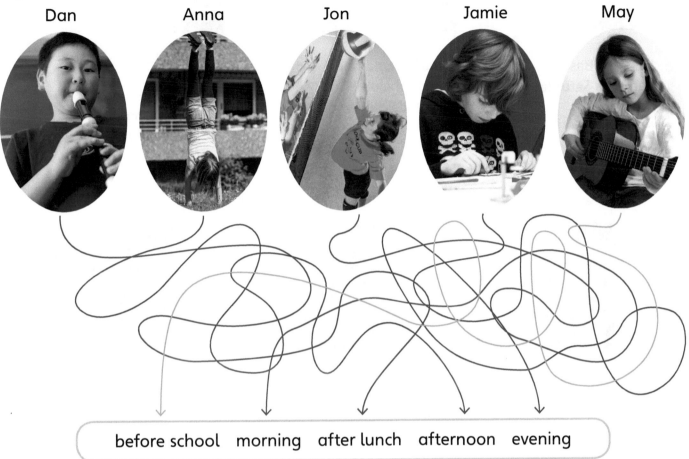

Dan   Anna   Jon   Jamie   May

before school   morning   after lunch   afternoon   evening

1 Dan plays the recorder before school.   *false*

2 Anna does gymnastics in the afternoon.   _____

3 Jon plays volleyball in the evening.   _____

4 Jamie makes models in the morning.   _____

5 May plays the guitar before school.   _____

5 **Look at activity 4. Complete the sentences.**

1 Dan *doesn't play the recorder* before school.

2 Anna _____ in the afternoon.

3 Jon _____ in the evening.

4 Jamie _____ in the morning.

5 May _____ before school.

6 **Look and read. Then answer the questions.**

Hi, Jack. Baseball game on Saturday morning.

Jack, remember model club is Tuesday afternoon. Ben

Hello, Jack. Don't forget gymnastics club Tuesday morning before school. Mom

Ella, see you Thursday evening for your piano lesson.

Hi, Ella. Don't forget movie club is Friday evening! Amy

Ella. Remember karate club Sunday morning. Dad

1 Does Jack play baseball on Saturdays?   _Yes, he does._

2 Does Ella play piano in the afternoon? _____

3 Does Jack make models in the evening? _____

4 Does Ella make movies on Sundays? _____

5 Does Jack do gymnastics before school? _____

6 Does Ella do karate on Sundays? _____

7 **Write questions about Jack and Ella.**

do gymnastics   make movies   make models
~~play the guitar~~   play the piano   play volleyball

1   _Does_   Jack   _play the guitar_ on Saturdays? No, he doesn't.

2 _____ Ella _____ on Thursdays? Yes, she does.

3 _____ Jack _____ on Tuesdays? Yes, he does.

4 _____ Ella _____ in the evening? Yes, she does.

5 _____ Jack _____ in the morning? Yes, he does.

6 _____ Ella _____ on Sundays? No, she doesn't.

Skills: *Writing*

8 **Read the paragraph and write the words.**

> after school   competitions   drink   hungry   ~~swimming~~   afternoon

My favorite sport is ¹ _swimming_ . I swim every Saturday and Sunday
² _____ . Sometimes there are ³ _____ . I'm always ⁴ _____
after swimming! I eat a sandwich and ⁵ _____ a glass of milk.
I enjoy playing tennis, too. We play ⁶ _____ on Friday.

9 (About Me) **Answer the questions.**

1 What is your favorite sport?

My favorite sport is _____

2 When do you do it?

_____

3 Are there any competitions?

_____

4 What do you eat and drink after playing sports?

_____

10 (About Me) **Write about your favorite sport.**

My favorite sport _____

_____

_____

_____

_____

_____

11 (About Me) **Ask and answer with a friend.**

> What's your favorite sport?   My favorite sport is horseback riding.

12 Read and number in order.

a

Good job, Lucas!

This is fun!

b

Hi, Lily. Come and play the guitar with me!

OK, great!

c

Where can we get a guitar?

Let's ask my cousin, Kim. She plays in a band.

1

d

Here, Lucas. Do you want to play the guitar, too?

No, I'm sorry. I can't play!

Come on, Lucas! Try it.

e

Practice every day, Lucas.

f

You can do it, Lucas! Like this …

Oh, dear!

13 Look at activity 12. Circle the answers.

1 Who plays in a band?
   a Tom's cousin   b Lily's cousin   c Lily

2 Who wants to play guitar with Kim?
   a Lily   b Anna   c Tom

3 What can't Lucas do?
   a play in a band   b find a guitar   c play the guitar

4 What is fun for Lucas?
   a watching Kim   b trying new things   c playing in a band

5 What does Kim want Lucas to do every day?
   a practice the guitar   b play in Kim's band   c try new things

14 Look and check the pictures that show the value: try new things.

15 Circle the words that sound like *sh*ark.

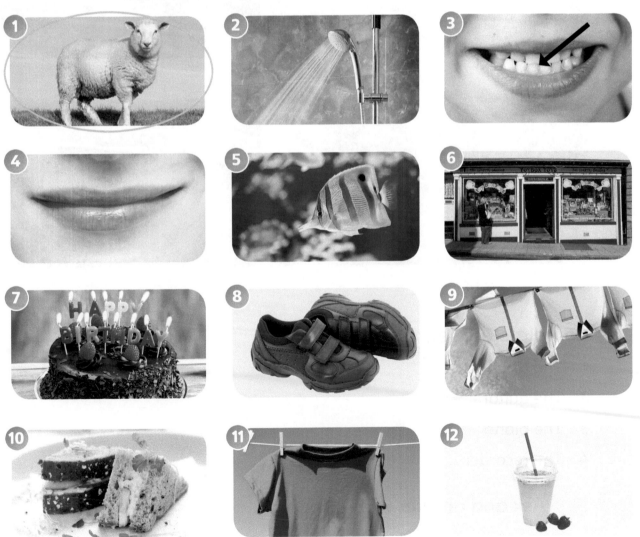

What type of musical instrument is it?

1 Look and guess. Then find and write the words.

girstn   srabs   sserciupon   ~~wwddinoo~~

woodwind

2 Complete the sentences.

1 The drum _____ *is a percussion instrument* .
2 The guitar _____ .
3 The piano _____ .
4 The recorder _____ .

3 (About Me) Ask and answer with a friend.

What instrument do you like?   I like the piano!

Evaluation

1 **Look and complete the Venn diagram. Then answer the questions.**

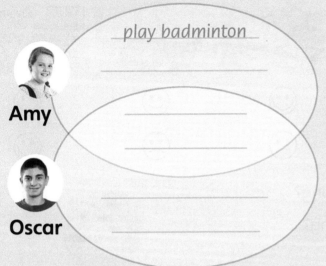

play badminton

Amy

Oscar

Day	Amy	Oscar
Monday morning		
Tuesday after school		
Thursday afternoon		
Friday evening		

1 Does Amy play the piano on Tuesdays? *Yes, she does.*

2 Does Oscar play the piano on Tuesdays? _____

3 Does Amy do karate on Fridays? _____

4 Does Oscar do karate on Tuesdays? _____

2 **Look at activity 1. Complete the sentences about Oscar.**

1 *He doesn't play* Ping-Pong after school.

2 _____ gymnastics on Wednesdays.

3 _____ karate in the morning.

4 _____ the piano on Fridays.

3 **Complete the sentences about this unit.**

1 I can talk about _____ .

2 I can write about _____ .

3 My favorite part is _____ .

4 **Guess what it is.**

Go to page 88 and circle the answer.

Review Units 5 and 6

1 **Look and answer the questions.**

Jade	☹	☺	☺	☺
Ben	☺	☹	☹	☺

1 Does Ben enjoy playing Ping-Pong? _Yes, he does._

2 Does Jade like playing Ping-Pong? _____

3 Does Ben like reading? _____

4 Does Jade love listening to music? _____

5 Does Ben enjoy playing the guitar? _____

6 Does Jade love playing the guitar? _____

Ben   Jade

2 **Look at activity 1. Complete the sentences.**

1 Jade loves _listening to music_, but she doesn't like _____ .

2 Ben enjoys _____ , but he doesn't like _____ .

3 Jade likes _____ , but she loves _____ .

4 Ben loves _____ , but he doesn't like _____ .

3 **(About Me) Answer the questions.**

1 Do you like playing Ping-Pong?

_____

2 Do you like playing the guitar?

_____

3 Do you like making lunch?

_____

4 Do you like washing clothes?

_____

4 (Think) **Look and write the verbs on the lists.**

do

1 *do your homework*
2 _____
3 _____

make

4 _____
5 _____
6 _____

play

7 _____
8 _____
9 _____

5 (About Me) **Look at activity 4. Write sentences.**

1 I _____ in the afternoon.

2 I _____ on Saturdays.

3 I like _____ , but _____ .

4 I enjoy _____ , but _____ .

7 At the market

1 Think Look and do the word puzzle.

Across →

1  2  3 

4  5  6 

Down ↓

7  8  9 

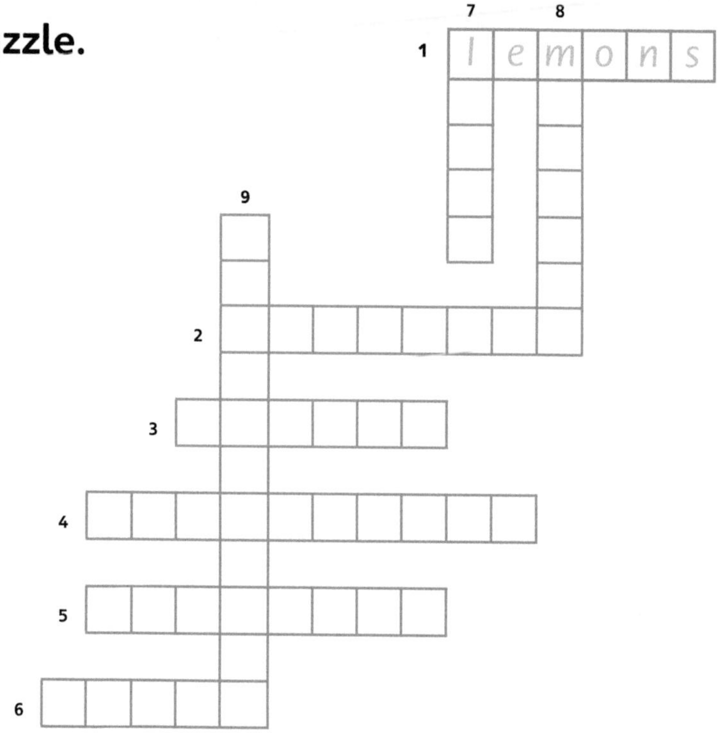

2 Think Circle the word that is different. Write a sentence about it.

1 lemons limes (onions) oranges — *Onions are vegetables.*

2 mangoes snails limes grapes ______

3 carrots peas pineapples ______

4 bananas pears sandwiches ______

3 About Me Answer the questions.

1 What's your favorite fruit?

My favorite ______

2 What color are they?

______

3 Are they big or small?

______

My picture dictionary → Go to page 86: Find and write the new words.

Read and circle the correct pictures.

1 There are lots of pineapples.

a    b    c

2 There are some onions.

a    b    c

3 There aren't any tomatoes.

a    b    c

4 There are lots of mangoes.

a    b    c

5 Think **Look and complete the sentences with *lots of*, *some*, or *not any*.**

1 There ____*aren't any*____ onions.

2 There _____ vegetables.

3 There _____ bananas.

4 There _____ tomatoes.

5 There _____ carrots.

6 Look and check *yes* or *no*.

	Yes, there are.	No, there aren't.
1 Are there any apples?	☐	✓
2 Are there any carrots?	☐	☐
3 Are there any mangoes?	☐	☐
4 Are there any beans?	☐	☐
5 Are there any watermelons?	☐	☐

7 Look at activity 6. Complete the questions and answers.

1 _____Are there any_____ grapes? _____Yes, there are._____

2 _____ coconuts? _____

3 _____ lemons? _____

4 _____ pineapples? _____

Skills: *Writing*

8 **Read the paragraph and write the words.**

> any   aren't   ~~favorite~~   juice   like   some

My ¹ _favorite_ smoothie is Tropical Yum. I like orange ² _____ .
It's in my favorite smoothie. Bananas are my favorite fruit. There are
³ _____ bananas in my smoothie. There aren't ⁴ _____ limes.
I don't ⁵ _____ them. They ⁶ _____ sweet.

9 (About Me) **Answer the questions.**

1 What's your favorite smoothie? Can you think of a name for it?
   My favorite smoothie is _____

2 Which juice do you like? Is it in your smoothie?
   _____

3 Make a list of the fruit in your smoothie.
   _____

4 What fruit don't you like in your smoothie?
   _____

10 (About Me) **Write about your favorite smoothie.**

My favorite smoothie _____
_____
_____
_____
_____
_____
_____

11 (About Me) **Ask and answer with a friend.**

What's your favorite smoothie?   My favorite smoothie is …

12 Read and write the words.

| are | has | ~~lots of~~ | red one | don't have |

There are ___lots of___ purses.

We _____ any money.

There _____ lots of old clothes in here.

Great! Let's look for a purse!

Yes! Look!

She _____ two purses!

Which purse do you want?

The _____ .

13 Look at activity 12. Circle the answers.

1 They're looking for a _____ .
    a purse   **b** guitar   **c** hat

2 They don't have any _____ .
    a shoes   **b** old clothes   **c** money

3 There are lots of _____ .
    a new clothes   **b** big clothes   **c** old clothes

4 Anna has _____ .
    a an old purse   **b** two purses   **c** two red purses

5 Lily wants the _____ .
    a blue purse   **b** red purse   **c** new purse

14 Look and check the pictures that show the value: reuse old things.

15 Draw the shapes around the words with the same sound.

☐ = sh ◯ = ch

What parts of plants can we eat?

1 **Look and guess. Then find and write the words.**

~~pragse~~ nabasan sepa insono torcars

grapes

2 **Look at activity 1. Read and complete the sentences.**

1 They're seeds. They're small. They're green. They're ___peas___ .

2 They're roots. They're orange. Rabbits like eating them. They're _____ .

3 They're purple fruit. We can't buy one. We buy lots of them. They're _____ .

4 They're stems. They're long. We don't eat them for breakfast. They're _____ .

5 They're yellow fruit. Monkeys enjoy eating them. They're _____ .

Evaluation

  Color the fruits and vegetables. Then answer the questions.

1 Are there any apples?   *Yes, there are.*

2 Are there any grapes?   _____

3 Are there any pears?   _____

4 Are there any watermelons?   _____

5 Are there any carrots?   _____

6 Are there any pineapples?   _____

 Write about your classroom.

> pencils   desks   flowers   ~~books~~   rabbits   windows

1 There are lots of ___*books*___ .

2 There are some _____ .

3 _____

4 _____

5 There aren't any _____ .

6 _____

  Complete the sentences about this unit.

1 I can talk about _____ .

2 I can write about _____ .

3 My favorite part is _____ .

  Guess what it is.

> Go to page 88 and circle the answer.

1 **Look and write the words. Then color the picture.**

1 Color the ___sun___ yellow.

2 Next to the towel is a _____ . Color it pink.

3 On the towel are some red and white _____ .

4 Can you see some _____ ? Color them blue.

2 **Find and circle. Then match and write the words.**

friesswimsuitoceantowelsandburger

___fries___

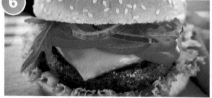

My picture dictionary ➡ Go to page 87: Find and write the new words.

3 (Think) **Look and write the words.**

hers   his   mine   ours   ~~theirs~~   yours

1 Which umbrella is _theirs_ ? The red one.

2 Which umbrella is _____ ? The purple one.

3 Which sock is _____ ? The white one.

4 Which sock is _____ ? The yellow one.

5 Which hat is _____ ?

6 The green one's _____ .

4 **Look and answer the questions.**

1 Which shell is his?

2 Which shell is hers?

3 Which towel is theirs?

4 Which towel is ours?

5 Which rabbit is mine?

The yellow one's his.

_____

_____

_____

_____

5 Think Look and circle the words.

Whose jacket is (that) / this?
(It's) / They're Ana's.

Whose shoes are these / those?
It's / They're theirs.

Whose bags are these / those?
It's / They're yours.

Whose sunglasses are these / those?
It's / They're mine.

Whose house is this / that?
It's / They're ours.

6 Look and complete the questions and answers.

Whose hat _is this_ ?

_It's_ his.

_____ bike _____ ?

_____ Tim's.

_____ paintings _____ ?

_____ mine.

_____ pencils _____ ?

_____ theirs.

Skills: *Writing*

7 **Read the postcard and answer the questions.**

1 Where is Dylan?
   At the beach.

2 What does he like doing in the morning?
   _____

3 Who does he enjoy playing with?
   _____

4 What does he do in the afternoon?
   _____

5 What does he eat for lunch?
   _____

> Dear Renata,
>   We are having a great vacation. We're at the beach.
>   I like flying my kite in the morning. I enjoy playing with my sister. In the afternoon, I swim in the ocean. It's great. There are lots of people swimming in the ocean. But there aren't any sharks. ☺
>   At lunchtime, we go to the café. I eat sausages and fries.
> See you soon,
> Dylan

8 (About Me) **Imagine you're on vacation. Answer the questions.**

1 Where are you? I'm _____

2 Who is on vacation with you? _____

3 What do you do in the morning? _____

4 What do you do in the afternoon? _____

5 What do you eat? _____

9 (About Me) **Write a postcard to a friend.**

Dear _____

I'm having a _____

_____

_____

_____

_____

10 **Ask and answer with a friend.**

What do you do on vacation?   I swim in the ocean.

11 Read and match.

1 Hi. Do you have my seven things?
2 Good idea. Let's ask my dad.
3 We hope you enjoy it!
4 Thank you, Mr. Lin.

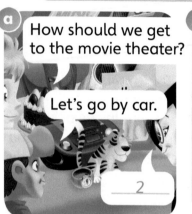

a How should we get to the movie theater?
Let's go by car.
2

b Wait a minute! Whose car is that?
It's Aunt Pat's.

c Aunt Pat!

d Welcome to our show!

12 Look at activity 11. Circle the answers.

1 Where do they go?
   a to the supermarket   **b** to the school   **c** to the movie theater

2 How do they get there?
   a by bike   **b** by car   **c** by bus

3 How many things do they have?
   a three   **b** five   **c** seven

4 Whose things are they?
   a Lily's   **b** Aunt Pat's   **c** Mr. Lin's

5 What are the things for?
   a family and friends   **b** Anna   **c** a show

13 Look and write the answers. Then check the picture that shows the value: appreciate your family and friends.

Thank you!   ~~Dinner is ready!~~   Five minutes, Mom!   You're a great dad!

1 Dinner is ready!

2 _____

14 Circle the words that sound like *dolphin*.

Are sea animals symmetrical?

1 **Look and write the words.**

jellyfish   octopus   crab   ~~shell~~   sea horse   starfish

shell

2 **Look at activity 1. Write about the sea animals.**

1   This shell is small. In this picture, the shell is symmetrical.

2   _____

3   _____

4   _____

5   _____

6   _____

Evaluation

1 Look and do the word puzzle.

Across **1**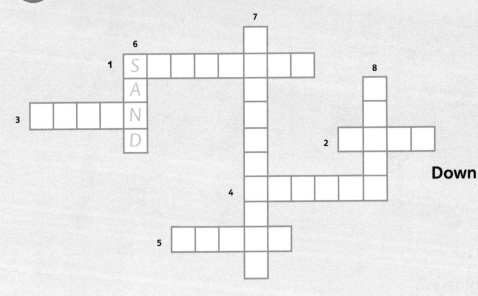

3 **4**

5

Down **6** **7**

8

Crossword grid:

```
            7
      6
   1  S □ □ □ □ □
      A                    8
3 □ □ N □            □
      D          2  □ □ □
                    □
            4 □ □ □ □ □ □
                    □
      5 □ □ □ □ □ □
                    □
```

2 (Think) Look and circle the answers.

1 Whose backpack is this? It's **hers** / (**his.**)

3 Which hat is his? It's the white one. / It's the red one.

2 Whose ball is this? It's **his** / **hers**.

4 Which jacket is hers? **It's the green one. / It's the blue one.**

3 (About Me) Complete the sentences about this unit.

1 I can talk about _____ .

2 I can write about _____ .

3 My favorite part is _____ .

4 (Puzzle) Guess what it is.

Go to page 88 and circle the answer.

Review Units 7 and 8

1 **Look and answer the questions.**

1	Are there any shorts?	*Yes, there are.*
2	Are there any sunglasses?	
3	Are there any shells?	
4	Is there a swimsuit?	
5	Is there a towel?	
6	Are there any pineapples?	
7	Are there any lemons?	
8	Is there a watermelon?	
9	Are there any onions?	
10	Are there any coconuts?	

2 **Look and match. Complete the sentences with *some*, *lots of*, or *not any*.**

1 *There are some* tomatoes.
2 _____ pears.
3 _____ lemons.
4 _____ shells.
5 _____ grapes.
6 _____ fries.

3 Look and circle the words.

1 Whose pineapple
is **this** / that?

It's / They're yours.

2 Whose onions are
these / those?

It's / **They're** yours.

3 Whose limes are
these / those?

It's / They're mine.

4 Whose shell is
this / that?

It's / They're mine.

4 (Think) Look and circle the words. Then answer the questions.

1 Which camera is **hers** / **yours**?

The small one's mine.

2 Which kite is **his** / **yours**?

_____

3 Which pencil case is **his** / **ours**?

_____

4 Which towel is **his** / **theirs**?

_____

5 Which bag is **hers** / **his**?

_____

5 Home time

do homework   watch TV   do the dishes   listen to music   wash the car
play on the computer   drink juice   make a cake   read a book   eat a sandwich

6 Hobbies

play the recorder   play Ping-Pong   do karate   play badminton   make models
play the guitar   make movies   play the piano   do gymnastics   play volleyball

7 At the market

onions   coconuts   watermelons   mangoes   pineapples
tomatoes   limes   pears   lemons   grapes

8 At the beach

swimsuit   fries   shells   sun   burger   sunglasses   sand   towel   ocean   shorts

My puzzle

1 Find the words ↓ →. Use the colored letters to answer the question.

P	G	P	I	B	R	A	R	Y	A	R	A	U	B
I	Q	L	R	T	G	Y	J	K	E	L	P	V	E
N	P	A	B	U	T	T	E	R	F	L	Y	U	V
E	B	Y	M	S	W	L	H	B	G	T	D	A	M
A	M	T	F	O	T	D	W	B	I	I	S	O	A
P	G	H	A	O	S	H	O	W	E	R	H	X	T
P	A	E	N	M	G	I	R	C	M	Q	E	Z	H
L	S	G	N	H	K	L	U	Y	O	O	L	P	M
E	M	U	A	E	T	R	E	R	E	S	L	L	Y
X	V	I	E	B	G	H	Y	O	P	W	F	R	Y
D	O	T	H	E	D	I	S	H	E	S	O	K	R
J	K	A	S	K	V	B	Y	U	W	E	T	R	E
M	L	R	W	T	E	C	J	F	G	A	N	N	A

Q: What are two fruits people can buy at the market?

A: _ _ _ _ _ _ _ and _ _ _ _ _ _

Thanks and Acknowledgements

Many thanks to everyone in the excellent team at Cambridge University Press. In particular we would like to thank Emily Hird, Liane Grainger, and Melissa Bryant whose professionalism, enthusiasm, experience, and talent makes them all such a pleasure to work with.

We would also like to give special thanks to Lesley Koustaff for her unfailing support, expert guidance, good humor, and welcome encouragement throughout the project.

The authors and publishers would like to thank the following contributors:
Blooberry Design: concept design, cover design, book design, page makeup
Charlotte Aldis: editorial training
Fiona Davis: editing
Lisa Hutchins: freelance editing
Ann Thomson: art direction, picture research
Gareth Boden Photography: commissioned photography
Ian Harker: audio recording
James Richardson: song and chant composition, arrangement of theme tune
Vince Cross: theme tune composition
John Marshall Media: audio recording and production
Phaebus: video production
hyphen S.A.: publishing management, American English edition

The authors and publishers acknowledge the following sources of copyright material and are grateful for the permissions granted. Although every effort has been made, it has not always been possible to identify the sources of all the material used, or to trace all copyright holders. If any omissions are brought to our notice, we will be happy to include the appropriate acknowledgments on reprinting.

The authors and publishers would like to thank the following illustrators:

Student's Book
Pablo Gallego: pp. 59, 60, 64, 69, 70, 74, 81, 82, 86, 91, 92, 96, 101; Luke Newell: pp. 61, 71, 83, 93; A Corazón Abierto: pp. 62, 84, 85, 94; Marcus Cutler: pp. 57, 79, 101.

Workbook
Pablo Gallego (Beehive Illustration): pp. 52, 60, 70, 78, 84; Gareth Conway (Bright Agency): pp. 50, 75, 83; Brian Lee: p. 54; Humberto Blanco (Sylvie Poggio): pp. 50, 56, 82; Simon Walmesley: pp. 64, 68, 74, 75, 83; A Corazón Abierto (Sylvie Poggio): pp. 48, 53, 65, 71, 79; Ilias Arahovitis (Beehive Illustration): pp. 55, 67, 73; Luke Newell: p. 49, 76; Marcus Cutler (Sylvie Poggio): pp. 53, 61; Graham Kennedy: p. 76; Monkey Feet: pp. 84, 85, 86, 87.

The authors and publishers would like to thank the following for permission to reproduce photographs:

Student's Book
p.87 (B/G): szefei/iStockphoto; p.65 (B/G): David Cayless/Getty Images; p.62 (TL): D. Hurst/Alamy; p.78 (CL): Tetra Images/Alamy; p.58–59: Adrian Cook/Alamy; p.62 (TR): Kim West/Alamy; p.63 (B/G): LanKS/Shutterstock, (L): Marc Debnam/Getty Images, (R): Ryan McVay/Getty Images; p.65 (BR): Joseph Van Os/Getty Images; p.66: Michael Marquand/Getty Images; p.67 (1)T: James Osmond/Alamy, (2)T: Mimadeo/iStockphoto, (3)T: isifa Image Service s.r.o./Alamy, (4)T: scenicireland.com/Christopher Hill Photographic/Alamy, (CL): AgStock Images, Inc/Alamy, (CR): incamerastock/Alamy, (BL): Scenics & Science/Alamy, (BC): Ingvar Bjork/Alamy; p.68–69: Tadej Zupancic/Getty Images; p.72 (TR): Edith Held/Corbis, (TC): Inti St Clair/Blend Images/Corbis, (TL): Zhelunovych/Shutterstock, (BR): AiVectors/Shutterstock; p.73 (B/G): nattanan726/Shutterstock, (R): Jose Luis Pelaez Inc/Getty Images, (BL): Erik Isakson/Getty Images; p.75 (B/G) & p.97 (B/G): Barry Downard, Getty Images; p.75 (BR): Denis Scott/Corbis, p.76: Richard T. Nowitz/Corbis; p.77 (1)T: Gary S. Chapman/Getty, (2)T: Rhythm Magazine/Getty Images, (3)T: Salvator Barki/Getty Images, (4)T: Mick Rowe/Getty Images, (5)T: IDREAMSTOCK/Alamy, (bugel): exopixel/Shutterstock, (tuba): the palms/Shutterstock, (drums): Kitch Bain/Shutterstock, (maracas): Discovod/Shutterstock, (harp): Ansis Klucis/Shutterstock, (guitar): Smileus/Shutterstock, (didgeridoo): Denys Kurylow/Shutterstock, (recorder): Myslitel/Shutterstock, (piano): Sergio Schnitzier/Shutterstock; page.78 (T): Terry Vine/Getty Images, (B): muzsy/Shutterstock, (CR): Radius Images/Alamy; p.80-81: Gonzalo Azumendi/Getty Images; p.85 (B/G): Valeri Potapova/Shutterstock, (T): Moxie Productions/Blend Images/Corbis, (BL): George Contorakes/Getty Images; p.87 (BR): Linda Freshwaters Arndt/Alamy; p.88: MIXA/Alamy; p.89 (TR): Filipe B. Varela/Shutterstock, (seed): BSIP SA/Alamy, (carrots) & p.99 (BR): S-F/Shutterstock; p.89 (potato): JIANG HONGYAN/Shutterstock, (peas): Yasonya/Shutterstock, (beans): Richard Griffin/Shutterstock, (tomatoes): vnlit/Shutterstock, (grapes): Africa Studio/Shutterstock, (lettuce): Crepesoles/Shutterstock, (spinach): photosync/Shutterstock, (asparagus): Dulce Rubia/Shutterstock, (onions): Preto Perola/Shutterstock; p.90–91: A bflo photo/Getty Images; p.95 (B/G): silvae/Shutterstock, (T) & (B): LOOK Die Bildagentur der Fotografen GmbH/Alamy; p.97 (BR): WaterFrame/Alamy; p.98: Dave Fleetham/Design Pics/Corbis; p.99 (1)T: aquapix/Shutterstock, (2)T: sunsinger/Shutterstock, (3)T: L. Powell/Shutterstock, (4)T: Stuart Westmorland/Corbis, (5)T: melissaf84,

(CL): Keith Tarrier/Shutterstock, (CR): Nedioimages/Photodisc/Getty Images, (BL): Vilaincrevette/Shutterstock; p.100 (TR): Henry Beeker/Alamy, (BL): Terry Mathews/Alamy, (BR): JTB MEDIA CREATION, Inc/Alamy, (C): Ivonne Wierink/Shutterstock; p.102: Elena Schweitzer/Shutterstock.

Commissioned photography by Gareth Boden: p.50 (T), (CL); p.53 (T); p.55 (project BR); p.61 (BL), (BR); p.65 (TL), (TR); p.67 (project BR); p.71 (BL), (BR); p. 75 (T); p.77 (project BR); p.84; p.87 (T); p.89 (project BR); p.94 (TL), (TR); p.97 (TL), (TR); p.99 (project BR).

Workbook
p. 48 (unit header): Adrian Cook/Alamy; p. 49 (photo a): p_ponomareva/Shutterstock; (photo b): Blend Images/Shutterstock; (photo c): Rido/Shutterstock; (photo d): MBI/Alamy; (photo e): © Deborah Vernon/Alamy; p. 51 (B/G): LanKS/Shutterstock; p. 54 (unit header): © Michael Marquand/Getty; (photo 1): antb/Shutterstock; (photo 2): Videowokart/Shutterstock; (photo 3): Boris Stroujko/Shutterstock; (photo 4): © dbimages/Alamy; p. 55 (TL, ML, BL): Sergey Novikov/Shutterstock; (TR, MR, BR): Goodluz/Shutterstock; (BR): Joe Cox/Shutterstock; p. 56 (unit header): Tadej Zupancic/Getty; (photo 1): George Doyle/Getty; (photo 2): p_ponomareva/Shutterstock; (photo 3): © Mikhail Kondrashov/fotomik/Alamy; (photo 4): Monkey Business Images/Shutterstock; p. 57 (photo 1): amana images inc./Alamy; (photo 2): © Westend61 GmbH/Alamy; (photo 3): © Prisma Bildagentur AG/Alamy; (photo 4): © Kenny Williamson/Alamy; (photo 5): wentus/Shutterstock; p. 58 (TL, TM, TR): Sombat Kapan/Shutterstock; (BL, BM, BR): Bipsun/Shutterstock; p. 59 (B/G): nattanan726/Shutterstock; p. 61 (photo 1): Tom Bird/Shutterstock; (photo 2): lendy16/Shutterstock; (photo 3): mikute/Shutterstock; (photo 4): ntstudio/Shutterstock; (photo 5): Anna Lurye/Shutterstock; (photo 6): © T.M.O.Buildings/Alamy; (photo 7): Romiana Lee/Shutterstock; (photo 8): Rob Hyrons/Shutterstock; (photo 9): Radka Tesarova/Shutterstock; (photo 10): Wiktory/Shutterstock; (photo 11): Mike Flippo/Shutterstock; (photo 12): M. Unal Ozmen/Shutterstock; p. 62 (unit header): © Richard T. Nowitz/Corbis; (photo 1): Yenwen Lu/Getty; (photo 2): © redsnapper/Alamy; (photo 3): © Bob Daemmrich/Alamy; (photo 4): Maxim Tarasyugin/Shutterstock; p. 63 (photo 1): Tatiana Popova/Shutterstock; (photo 2): Mendelex/Shutterstock; (photo 3): Vereshchagin Dmitry/Shutterstock; (photo 4): Attl Tibor/Shutterstock; (photo 5): bogdan ionescu/Shutterstock; (photo 6): Erik Isakson/Getty; (photo 7): Attl Tibor/Shutterstock; (photo 8): Vereshchagin Dmitry/Shutterstock; (photo 9): cristovao/Shutterstock; (photo 10): eurobanks/Shutterstock; (photo 11): EKS design/Shutterstock; p. 64: Edith Held/Corbis; p. 66 (unit header): © Gonzalo Azumendi/Getty; (photo 1): Candus Camera/Shutterstock; (photo 2): Daniel M Ernst/Shutterstock; (photo 3): George Dolgikh/Shutterstock; (photo 4): sjk2012/Shutterstock; (photo 5): Mukesh Kumar/Shutterstock; (photo 6): Antonova Anna/Shutterstock; (photo 7): IngridHS/Shutterstock; (photo 8): Nataliya Arzamasova/Shutterstock; (photo 9): BrazilPhotos/Shutterstock; p. 67 (BR): Aleksandar Mijatovic/Shutterstock; p. 69 (B/G): Valeri Potapova/Shutterstock; p. 71 (photo 1): nodff/Shutterstock; (photo 2): yykkaa/Shutterstock; (photo 3): Matt9122/Shutterstock; (photo 4): CREATISTA/Shutterstock; (photo 5): Africa Studio/Shutterstock; (photo 6): GoodMood Photo/Shutterstock; p. 72 (unit header): © MIXA/Alamy; (photo 1): Fabio Bernardi/Shutterstock; (photo 2): bergamont/Shutterstock; (photo 3): Kuttelvaserova Stuchelova/Shutterstock; (photo 4): Kesu/Shutterstock; (photo 5): Jiri Hera/Shutterstock; p. 73 (BR): Kozub Vasyl/Shutterstock; p. 74 (unit header): © Abflo photo/Getty; (photo 1): © foodfolio/Alamy; (photo 2): Denis Tabler/Shutterstock; (photo 3): ankiro/Shutterstock; (photo 4): K. Miri Photography/Shutterstock; (photo 5): Slavica Stajic/Shutterstock; (photo 6): stockcreations/Shutterstock; p. 77 (B/G): silvae/Shutterstock; p. 79 (photo 1): Juergen Faelchle/Shutterstock; (photo 2): Maryna Kulchytska/Shutterstock; (photo 3): Kondrachov Vladimir/Shutterstock; (photo 4): Donovan van Staden/Shutterstock; (photo 5): jannoon028/Shutterstock; (photo 6): Studio 1231/Shutterstock; (photo 7): Andrey Armyagov/Shutterstock; (photo 8): Rocketclips, Inc./Shutterstock; (photo 9): Bloomua/Shutterstock; p. 80 (unit header): © Dave Fleetham/Design Pics/Corbis; (photo 1): Lucy Liu/Shutterstock; (photo 2): Evocation Images/Shutterstock; (photo 3): QiuJu Song/Shutterstock; (photo 4): Olga Desyatun/Shutterstock; (photo 5): Vittorio Bruno/Shutterstock; (photo 6): Cuson/Shutterstock; p. 81 (photo 1): Dan Fairchild Photography/Getty; (photo 2): Mirek Kijewski/Shutterstock; (photo 3): Songchai W/Shutterstock; (photo 4): Photodisc/Getty; (photo 5): pyzata/Shutterstock; (photo 6): OliverSved/Shutterstock; (photo 7): Littlehenrabi/Shutterstock; (photo 8): Elena Shashkina/Shutterstock; (photo 9): Cherry-Merry/Shutterstock; (photo 10): © Steve Skjold/Alamy; (BR): ZiZ7StockPhotos/Shutterstock; p. 82 (photo 1): Filip Fuxa/Shutterstock; (photo 2): Givaga/Shutterstock; (photo 3): Lessimol/Shutterstock; (photo 4): Tei Sinthipsomboon/Shutterstock; (photo 5): Dutourdumonde Photography/Shutterstock; (photo 6): Anna Biancoloto/Shutterstock; p. 88 (puzzle header): StepanPopov/Shutterstock.

Our special thanks to the following for their kind help during location photography:

Barratt Developments PLC; Queen Emma Primary School

Front Cover photo by Sylvestre Machado/Getty Images